Contents

Introduction

From Tara

I often say there is no writing poetry. There is only co-writing poetry, and the co-writer is a mysterious force and source that I cannot name.

When I write poetry, I begin by listening, listening to what wants to come through. It requires my full attention, a kind of straining and effort to make out the words through some fog. The co-writer leads.

Later in the process, I play a more active role—revising, tightening, listening for patterns of rhythm and sound and making them stronger. That's the part of the poetic craft our conscious minds can handle. The real source of the poems is something much wiser than my conscious mind and much more expansive than my personality-self.

After writing poems for a year or so, I looked back over all the poems I had written, wondering: is there some theme? Some point of connection?

I saw that many of the poems offered a different way of seeing ourselves. They offered, quite literally, "other names" to call ourselves. They said, *you are not actually "Susan" or "Mark" or Jane" – or whatever your given name may be. You are something else.*

One poem asks the reader to remember their other name as this: "Strong cauldron for the feast of light."

Another asks,

Can you feel the one
deep inside your chest
who has existed forever?
Who has made a thousand journeys?
Who feels like a comet in the dark?
The inner filament?

I know, no one ever told you.
I know. It wasn't the name you learned to write at school,
but that one is you.
That one is the real you.

I've begun to see that the poems each offer some alternative way to conceive of ourselves, distinct from our culture's normative idea of self. The concept of self that most of us were raised with and walk around with is that the self is the ego: defined by a name, a set of attributes (profession, family roles, place of residence, personality strengths and weaknesses, physical appearance); and by a narrative of life events (I grew up here, went to school there, then did this, then that).

The problem? As so many of the world's wisdom traditions have articulated, seeing ourselves only as this is a recipe for angst, anxiety and discontent. This concept of identity is partial, and in some sense, false.

When we locate our identity in the ego, we end up run by a litany of likes and dislikes about ourselves and our lives. We start to relate to ourselves as concepts—characters—rather than as beings having an experience in this moment. We behave in all kinds of harmful ways as we seek to shape that self-concept and "defend" it from perceived threats.

In my own life, when I think of myself simply as "Tara"— the 5'0" married woman from San Francisco who writes and teaches classes, etcetera—there is a narrow, self-critical tone to my life experience. I'm filled with thoughts of what I'd like to change about what is. I am more irritable with those I love. There is a pressure to get it right, to live up to a picture of how I think my life should be.

There is another way of being. That other way includes my identity as Tara, but holds it in the context of "my other names," identities that are far more mysterious, subtle, fluid. That other state of being allows me to remember that I am more a field of shifting energies than I am a stable "self." That other way remembers that I am a permeable cell within a greater organism—humanity, life, earth—rather than a separate entity.

When I dip into these other names, I experience a kind of freedom, an expansiveness, and most dear to me, a peaceful sanity—a liberation from the discontent.

I believe that, for our sanity, for our happiness, we all need ways into our other names.

Meditation is one way in. Immersive experiences—from painting to dancing to writing—in which we become one with what we are doing, are another tool.

Poetry provides another route. Poems that speak to and from our other names can help us find our way through the noise of the world, and the noise of our minds, to those deeper layers of who we are.

Poetry can also become practice. In my own life, and in my work with students around their other names, we ask: "If you see yourself as 'a strong cauldron for the feast of light' in this moment, how does that change the complaints you have against your body? How does it change how you are approaching this meeting? How does it shift the irritation you feel at so and so?"

"If you connect with 'the inner filament, the one that feels like a comet in the dark,' how does this difficult relationship look different? If you remember in this moment that you are not a separate self, but 'a limb of the earth,' what changes?"

We can use the imagery and sounds of poetry to help us remember and connect to our other names.

May the words that follow find resonance within. May they find their way to your heart. May they help you remember your true name.

Love,
Tara

Poems

Your Other Name

If your life doesn't often make you feel
like a cauldron of swirling light –

If you are not often enough a woman standing
above a mysterious fire,
lifting her head to the sky –

You are doing too much, and listening too little.

Read poems. Walk in the woods. Make slow art.
Tie a rope around your heart, be led by it off the plank,
happy prisoner.

You are no animal. You are galaxy with skin.
Home to blue and yellow lightshots,
making speed-of-light curves and racecar turns,
bouncing in ricochet –

Don't slow down the light and turn it into matter
with feeble preoccupations.

Don't forget your true name:
Presiding one. Home for the gleaming.
Strong cauldron for the feast of light.

Strong cauldron for the feast of light:
I am speaking to you.
I beg you not to forget.

The One Deep Inside Your Chest

Step back and watch your body, being a body.
Watch an arm move through space, watch an ankle turn.

Watch your body, as it likes things or doesn't,
as it gets scrapes and bruises
as the skin darkens and falls into folds.

Step back to the perimeter of the theater
and watch your body on the stage.

Recede to that quiet knowing:
For now, I am associated with this body –
not inside it, or one with it –
just associated, for a time.

Casing. Only casing.
Be kind to the casing if you like –
put oils on it and nourish it and move it
to keep it stronger, for a time.
Never become it. There, only suffering.

Can you feel the one deep inside your chest,
who has existed forever?
Who has made a thousand journeys?
Who feels like a comet in the dark?
The inner filament?

I know, no one ever told you.
I know. It wasn't the name you learned to write at school,
but that one is you.
That one is the real you.

The Ending of the Odyssey

Oh angel, messenger,
face in the mirror –

Something keeps asking me
to see my face.
Something waits for me,
is waiting for a meeting
I am busy putting off.

But when this odyssey has reached its end,
you will know it by my face:
clear like a porcelain bowl,
lenient and tender,
round as humility,
All open, all true.

My face will curve itself
around gravity toward you.
And you – angel, messenger, long lost friend –
will silk my cheek to your palm.

All is forgiven.
All floats like air and streams like water.
All tumbles down into the river of compassion.

Then we'll meet one another, all of us, in the field,
and, turning northward,
decide to take the long way home.

The Quiet Power

I walked backwards, against time
and that's where I caught the moon
singing at me.

I steeped downwards, into my seat
and that's where I caught freedom
waiting for me like a lilac.

I ended thought, and I ended story.
I stopped designing, and arguing, and
sculpting a happy life.

I didn't die. I didn't turn to dust.

Instead I chopped vegetables,
and made a calm lake in me
where the water was clear and sourced and still.

And when the ones I loved came to it,
I had something to give them, and
it offered them a soft road out of pain.

I became beloved.

And I came to know that this was it.
The quiet power.
I could give something mighty, lasting,
that stopped the wheel of chaos,

by tending to the river inside,
keeping the water rich and deep,
keeping a bench for you to visit.

In the End

In the end
you won't be known
for the things you did,
or what you built,
or what you said.

You won't even be known
for the love given
or the hearts saved,

because in the end you won't be known.

You won't be asked, by a vast creator full of light:
What did you do to be known?

You will be asked: Did you know it,
this place, this journey?

What there is to know can't be written.
Something between the crispness of air
and the glint in her eye
and the texture of the orange peel.

What you'll want a thousand years from now is this:
a memory that beats like a heart–
a travel memory, of what it was to walk here,
alive and warm and textured within.

Sweet brightness, aliveness, take-me-now-ness that is life.

You are here to pay attention. That is enough.

The Last Word

There could be this other way, she said, of living from the
inside out.

Really doing it, she meant.

Letting go of, "I am she, of this name.
Of this home, and marriage, and weight.
Of this conduct. Of these beliefs, and not those."

Instead, she said, it could be like this:
I weave at the river. I speak with fish.
When I stand at the water, the sun is in my chest.
The woods walk me home.

Most of the things I know have no words,
but I need none, *for I am them.*

On my last day, memory will be a blazing orange sunset,
and I'll rest in the sling of the horizon.

The last word on my lips will be *member:*
I was a member of this, a limb of it.

I was *that* blessed -- to be a limb of it.

I Never Believed in Death

I never believed in death, for I never saw it.

I saw only that this became that.
The petals fell away, and the thing became a stem,
and the floor became scattered in pink.

Containers break. Eras end.
Thing-ness only a stopping ground,
a pause at the train station, followed by moving on.

You were never yourself, and I was never I.
Everything cresting and falling,
giving way, again, to the ocean.

When you know you are just a disco party
of cells that came together for a time,
you'll live like the blazing sphere you are,
and dance with the spheres around you.

You won't ask of them, or tax them,
or want them to be anything.

You'll be boogieing in the sun, and look
over your shoulder, breathless, to say

Quick! It's only for a moment that we are this.
Let's watch our knees glisten
As we land from a raucous jump.
Let's wait and watch our hands darken
Covered with night.

Let's cry, at the realness of it,
and the dreamness of it,
for a time.

Birthday Wish

sun moss wildflowers
trees shade dirt
roots wishes seagulls

silence with birds
and laughter against stones
and circles of laughter
and belly everything

and time with the reeds
and pictures with sky
and sun christening

and surrender and surrender and surrender
to the body I am.

surrender to all this,
to the lusciousness I forgot.

wholeness rising up, still here.

Summer

It was a summer of loganberries
of lake ripples and sky light,
rough grain of the couch beneath my thigh.

Summer of pondering leaves
and patience before a worm, for its secrets.

Summer of praying at altars of berries,
and lying across sea rocks, asking of them.

Of communion and tears,
homecoming to the one I had lost,
the humming earth.

Fierce waves beat off my sadness.
Sand scrubbed the withering from my face.
Only sea glint remained, all the pain burned off.
That's one thing
the sun is for, you know:
to bake pain.

And the wind, to strip it away,
and the sand, to buff the final shards into shimmer.

After all that,
an estranged happiness arose
and a space from which I could see the astonishment of green.
I could let it make me weep, and be blessed by it.

The thought occurred: perhaps like this,
if I could remember this,
I could do less harm.
I could inhabit humbly.

Perhaps I could even offer something–
be like a berry, or a vine, to the world.

Awakening

Buff off routine. Polish away habit.
Sharpen your crystal mind with silent time.
Wake yourself by praying to the gods.

Surrender all of image. Let go of your outside eyes.
Be a foolish animal, gaping at the forest.
Be clumsy and too much and wide-eyed.

Kill the thing that pulls back the reins,
and run.

The Real Life

Don't be greedy with the universe, she said to me.

But she didn't say it in the mean way.
She didn't say don't dream big, don't want things, don't think
you deserve.

She meant: look at your life and trust it.
Notice how you have forever been given what you need.

Notice how, while you've been railing and ranting and wanting,
enoughness has gathered around you like stones around a fire,

How, while you've been making lists of what should be
wishing the set and costumes were different,
there was a whole other play happening on another stage.

The real life.

Witnessed when you hand a dollar
to the woman behind the register
in the color of an orange
in the magic laugh

Never calling, just crackling, speaking in tones —
the real life

Cup your hands and ask for it.
Start looking.
Sweetness. Honey in a bowl. Nectar.

Solitude

You can learn to keep yourself company,
but only by keeping yourself company —

Do you ask "how are you?" and listen
like a deer deciphering a rustling in the leaves?

Do you say "take a walk with me, and let me show you the woods?"

Do you sing yourself a song?

Now *you* are the one: the one to care
for all the whispers inside
the one to listen to all the children within,
to take them to see beautiful places and new sights.

That's you: the woman leading the field trip,
the woman making hot chocolate for all of them,
the woman saying, "now, now, that's enough."

If you feel like an incomplete circle, or a wilted form
go home to silence and listen to yourself.

Give your words a hearing.
Shine each pebble and dagger to the light.
Meet each with lilac compassion.

Your own sweet song
will overtake your life and blaze
so loud you need an earth
this listening to hold it.

Contentment springs up,
again and again, from the well
where you least expected to discover it.

The Inner Whistling

They forgot to tell me too

that there was always this whistle,
this reed, making quiet music.

It moved like a woman
making her way
through a crowd
like a ship tacking
this way and that
on the sea.

It was the beginning of me
and the very *me of me*
and I became a stranger to it.

But when the mountain came tumbling down,
I knelt at a window and wept.
A small bird, blue like skylight
offered me milk and cookies
and sang into my weeping.

Then I fell into the hammock of the ancient moon
and a book began to write itself.
The pen was my keeper
and the page was my face
and the craft was yours, my god.

Dreamkeeper, Sleepweaver, Elegance of all:
I kneel to you. I sew your skin.
I wait at the road for your arrivals.
I return. I return. I return.

Coming Home

The warmth of the hearth in my chest
and the breath of warm enoughness
and something like love in my throat,
a dense goodness covering –

all this: because I am home.

Because I fought the fight,
as difficult as Odysseus' journey.
I slayed dragons, and scaled steep peaks,
laid down in a bed with fear,
and walked through the woods in the night.

A thousand trials to get home.

Yet the journey was also
Dorothy clicking her heels three times,
being instantly transported there,
Homecoming like rain, like grace—
without struggle or trial or mud.

The long road and the non-road home.
It's as simple as knocking and as far
as a thousand miles to get there.

In that home place, I can see:
nothing was ever broken.

Warmth savors up from our chests like a hearth
and love is in our throats, lunging outward,
and the world is a basket of gifts,
and we sit in it, just sit,
and tears rise, at the intensity of it.

Problemlessness

Beyond the cackling of the birds
and all the fighting, and all the noise–
What else is here?

The oak tree's heart, which says:
Glory is. Wholeness is.
And unavoidably, my dear, you are a part of it.

Problemlessness. I know – you couldn't hear it before,
but I'm asking you now – to go inside the oak,
and wait –

till your heart is wrenched by its love
and you see no need for language

till your hands are cupped receiving
and everything comes to you baked in lovesilence

There is no name for what enters you then.
Everything is a red sun rising
and everywhere an infinite grace before you

Then there is no name for what you become –
like love, like the mountain.

The Rhythm

In any creative feat
(by which I mean your work, your art, your life)
there will be downtimes.

Or so it seems.
Just as the earth is busy before the harvest
and a baby grows before its birth,
there is no silence in you.
There is no time of nothingness.

What if,
during the quiet times,
when the idea flow is hushed and hard to find
you trusted (and yes I mean trusted)
that the well was filling, the waters moving?

What if you trusted
that for the rest of eternity,
without prodding, without self-discipline,
without getting over being yourself,
you would be gifted every ounce of productivity you need?
What would leave you? What would open?

And what if during the quiet times you ate great meals
and leaned back to smile at the stars,
and saw them there, as they always are,
nourishing you?

There are seasons and harvest
is only a fraction of one of them.

There is the rhythm that made everything.
The next time you stand in the kitchen, leaning,
the next time a moment of silence catches you there,
hear it, that rhythm, and let it place a stone in your spine.
Let it bring you some place beautiful.

Axis

Each one hikes her life
around her axis of mystery.

You are here only because
the cells balanced in some dark place,
the cells found each other in some dark place.

You were some mind's long journey
before you became the one that takes the journey.

You were miracles in the making
before you became the one whose palms bounce miracles
like children bounce jacks on the gray sidewalk.

Turn Your Palm

I invited you in to the mystery with an open hand.
I invited you in to the lap of love.
I walked you down a golden path
and touched your eyelids when you slept.

Then I turned away
and showed you a darker moon.
You live in the land of bothness;
without lost you can't know found.

You stumbled like a lost, numb one.
You passed on pain:
covered another's mouth,
raised an elbow against their cheek,
said "No, not that. Not you."

It begins like that. It doesn't begin
with an atom bomb or a vicious fight.
It begins with a small silver needle
that sews its way through and
says, I block this.
I do not want to hear that word.
I do not want to see that face.
I am against.

Instead:
Curve around it. Curve around everything.
Turn your palm over and become a listening bowl.

Yes: this will turn your convictions to dust
and feel like a slicing death.

What is dying is your prison.

Whatever you hear, let your heart
be a golden sieve to it.

The Visitor

The old dream gave way to the new dream,
because the new dream grew up and grew out,
and waited at the window black against the sky,
like branches of an oak.

The old dream didn't end or crumble into wrinkles.
It simply slipped into darkness and found another home.

Each of us containers of dreams for a time
visited by them, houseguests
hovering where the ceiling meets the wall,
painting at the edges of our lives.

We are reluctant hosts:
don't interrupt my plans, my certainty
don't ask that of me
don't upend the teacups
don't open that window to the wind
don't make me crack the fear in my back
like that.

Most of us live with the hoverers like this,
turning over our shoulders, again and again, saying:
You again? Still hovering? Not moving on yet?
Can I sweep you out with a broom?

Sauce bubbling on the stove
and teenagers at the table
and damp socks and the dog passing through
and then you: otherworldly thing,
asking, whispering, planting seeds –

I keep watch on you, and you on me.
I'm not sure how to bring you down to the floor.
There's no braiding you in, or "incorporating" you,
for you would lead me out of this house

to a violet moon and black stars.

Maybe in the end, all the rest will be erased
and my life will be recorded as a dialogue with you.

Maybe the rest is a theater of noise,
and this conversation I can barely name
will come forth in ink, the real story of my life.

And maybe we were dancing elsewhere,
even as I stirred soup on the stove.
Maybe I also lived under the violet moon.

I never thought I was only located here.
And how I suffered, when I thought I was.

Courage

It wasn't against the stone
or with the morning
that it rose.

It wasn't in the night
or from the breakers
that it came to me.

It wasn't whistling in a nest
or hiding in the breeze.
None of that.

It was a dark coal
that had grown silent
and one day, came to light.

Why did the coal alight?

Perhaps from pain, because pain
climbs until it snaps--

Perhaps because someone listened,
and listened wholly--

Perhaps because a flashing spark
flew in and whispered the truth
at your neck, as sparks so often do.

How *else* could courage come?

Courage born of love, not bravery

Courage: making the canal wide with love
when life would squeeze it thin.

Courage only as wide as love,

can only water as much as love is in the jar.

You can invite her to your table
and bring apples and grapes and wine,
and ask her to stay forever.
She'll only smile, silver eyes hovering
 and say:

You don't have to grasp me.
No fist. No lock. No beekeeper's net.

Store me in a dark closet somewhere.
I don't mind being shut away,
among coat hems and rain boots.

I am happy to wait, and counsel spirits,
run strength up the walls,
while you can the apples
and feed the children
and stare at a patient moon.

Or else pack her somewhere, deep in your back
behind a kidney, or below a hidden rib,
and watch how she changes your spine.

Let her move through you, when you need her,
like a sword, like a firerush
like a wish for the world

like something soft and fluttering
offered up from your hand.

Art-Making Poem

Your gifts are shy,
and stand behind you, like a child
peeking out from mommy's leg.

But you already know that.

You've seen it a thousand times
as you tucked and buried them
wondering what was wrong with you

It wasn't *you*. Gifts are bashful.
Most live hidden, and
die in alleys or crumble into broken stones.

What to do?

*How to entice them to open the sliding door
and step out?*

A mad love for the thing itself
is the best remedy that's been discovered

a love so wild you are willing to step
into the middle of a circle and dance.

You won't know if the witnesses around you
are the neighbors
or the world
or just the critics from within

but you'll go there
for the feeling of your foot sanding the floor,
for the flight in your chest when you jump.

That's the best prescription:
a kind of foolery, a mad love.

But what if the fear has won out, you ask?

First, sink down to the floor and kiss
your feet.

Fall like someone has just
popped the balloon of you.

Then hug yourself into stillness.
Know that, sweetie, it will be alright.

Next build a fort in your bedroom,
a soft and covered space.
Pitch blankets, prop pillows,
bring a firefly inside for light.

Then take it out, whatever it is
your flute or your pen or your clay,
and say your prayer of thank you
for this everything: vessel for your thoughts,
ceaseless companion, adventure-bringer, peace song.

Then take the question, Is it good or not?
and send it to the river to fish.
Let it catch you dinner while you work.

You are not making to be good.
You are making because
it is the great romance of your life.

Then make something. A little thing.
Look at how it loves you
how it woke up the earth to you
and gave you the life-heart back

how the days are growing long again, as in childhood,
as if time is being given back to you
as you learn how your soul wants to fill it.

.

Benedictions

You-Shaped Hole

Sometimes the world feels inhospitable.
You feel all the ways that you and it don't fit.
You see what's missing, how it all could be different.

You feel as if you weren't meant for the world, or the world
wasn't meant for you.

As if the world is "the way it is" and your discomfort
with it a problem.

So you get timid. You get quiet about what you see.

But what if this? What if you are meant
to feel the world is inhospitable, unfriendly, off-track
in just the particular ways that you do?

The world has a you-shaped hole in it.
It is missing what you see.
It lacks what you know.

And so you were called into being.
To see the gap, to feel the pain of it, and to fill it.

Filling it is speaking what is missing.
Filling it is stepping into the center of the crowd,
into a clearing, and saying,
here, my friends, is the future.
Filling it is being what is missing, becoming it.

You don't have to do it all, but you do have to speak it.
You have to tell your slice of the truth.
You do have to walk toward it with your choices,
with your own being.

Then allies and energies will come to you like fireflies swirling
around a light.

The roughness of the world, the off-track-ness,
the folly that you see,
these are the most precious gifts
you will receive in this lifetime.

They are not here to distance you from the world,
but to guide you into your contribution to it.

The world was made with a you-shaped hole in it.
In that way you are important.
In that way you are here to make the world.
In that way you are called.

Love Poem

There are the ones who know how to love,
who sit in the mirror of each other's eyes
and find the basket of forever.

There are the ones who step with joy,
and make the earth cheerful beneath their feet.
Their home is a field of golden poppies,
old laughters pile into every corner and
joy runs down the hall like a brook.

Visitors say: this is a place
we would want to go, should we ever
fall sick and need to get well again,
should we ever fall lost, and need
to remember what it is to be strong or true.

Even Time came there, and knelt
in the garden in stillness,
and enamored, forgot His work,
becoming one of the happy vines.

In silences, they said to one another:
How you find me.
How you stay.
How this thing renews itself,
How delight keeps growing up, like a vine, at our table.

We didn't know we might be able to do this:
put up the circus tent, laugh a thousand times,
make everything a weaving, circling, partner dance.

This Is Your Time

This is your time.

Your time to say what you have kept silent.

Your time to ask your big questions without apology.

Your time to shine like a blazing comet,
whether they like it or not.

Your time to believe what your heart tells you:
that this world could be very different.

Your time to live by your rhythms,
and teach them to the world.

Your time to nurture your village back to health.

Your time to show the world what it has been missing.

Your time to show the world the other side of itself.

Even in the Struggle

Even in the struggle, you are loved.
You are being loved not in spite of the hardship, but through it.
The thing you see as wrenching, intolerable,
life's attack on you,
is an expression of love.

There is the part of us that fears and protects
and defends and expects,
and has a story of the way it's supposed to turn out.
That part clenches in fear, feels abandoned and cursed.

There is another part, resting at the floor
of the well within, that understands:
this is how I am being graced, called, refined, by fire.

The secret is, it's all love.
It's all doorways to truth.
It's all opportunity to merge with what is.

Most of us don't step through the doorframe.
We stay on the known side.
We fight the door, we fight the frame, we scream and hang on.

On the other side, you are one
with the earth, like the mountain.
You hum with life, like the moss.
On the other side, you are more beautiful:
wholeness in your bones, wisdom in your gaze,
the sage-self and the surrendered heart alive.

Things We Don't Know Yet

How to create a childhood worthy
of the sacredness of the child

How to forgive ourselves, entirely

How to love without projection or dependence

How to honor the strength of love
alongside the strength of might

How much we are held, blessed

What we would create, if we believed we could

We're still young, still in an early era.

The status quo is just a middle chapter.

So have compassion for this fools' world of ours

and don't be afraid

to be the one

to help us turn the page.

About Tara

Tara Sophia Mohr is a writer and personal growth teacher. Her work on spirituality, well-being and women's leadership has been featured on *The Today Show, Huffington Post, Whole Living, Forbes, Ode Magazine, Big Think, Beliefnet, CNN.com,* and numerous other publications. She is the creator of the Playing Big leadership program for women and of the popular 10 Rules for Brilliant Women Workbook.

Tara received her MBA from Stanford University and her undergraduate degree in English Literature from Yale. She lives in San Francisco, California.

www.taramohr.com

Art Credits

Cover Image: *Ablaze* by Tracey Clark

Untitled, Susannah Conway, p.17
Letting Go, Tracey Clark, p.20
Ablaze, Tracey Clark, p.24
Pretty Things, Tracey Clark, p.28
Leaving Harbour, Christa Gallopoulos, p.32
Untitled, Susannah Conway, p.37
Twinkle Lights, Tracey Clark, p.40
Untitled, Tracey Clark, p.50
A Place To Land, Christa Gallopoulos, p.52

To view more of Tracey Clark's work, visit:
www.traceyclark.com

To view more of Susannah Conway's work, visit:
www.susannahconway.com

To view more of Christa Gallopoulos's work, visit:
www.carryitforward.com

Book design by Adele Miller, visit:
www.dellie.ca

Made in the USA
Lexington, KY
11 October 2013